GOD'S MESSY
FAMILY

FINDING YOUR PLACE WHEN LIFE ISN'T PERFECT

JACOB ARMSTRONG

Abingdon Press
Nashville

GOD'S MESSY FAMILY
FINDING YOUR PLACE WHEN LIFE ISN'T PERFECT

Library of Congress Cataloging-in-Publication Data has been requested.

ISBN 978-1-5018-4356-3

18 19 20 21 22 23 24 25 26 27—10 9 8 7 6 5 4 3 2 1
MANUFACTURED IN THE UNITED STATES OF AMERICA

To Phoebe—

Thanks for all the stories we have written together.
I look forward to a million more.

God's Messy Family
Finding Your Place When Life Isn't Perfect

God's Messy Family
978-1-5018-4356-3
978-1-5018-4357-0 eBook

God's Messy Family: Leader Guide
978-1-5018-4358-7
978-1-5018-4359-4 eBook

God's Messy Family: DVD
978-1-5018-4360-0

The Connected Life:
Small Groups That Create Community

This handy and helpful guide describes how churches can set up, maintain, and nurture small groups to create a congregation that is welcoming and outward-looking. Written by founding pastor Jacob Armstrong with Rachel Armstrong, the guide is based on the pioneering small group ministry of Providence United Methodist Church in Mt. Juliet, Tennessee.

978-1-5018-4345-7
978-1-5018-4346-4 eBook

Also by Jacob Armstrong:
A New Playlist: Hearing Jesus in a Noisy World (The Connected Life Series)
Interruptions: A 40-Day Journey with Jesus
Loving Large
Renovate: Building a Life with God (The Connected Life Series)
The God Story
Treasure: A Four-Week Study on Faith and Money
Upside Down

With Jorge Acevedo:
Sent: Delivering the Gift of Hope at Christmas

With James W. Moore:
Christmas Gifts That Won't Break: Expanded Edition with Devotions

With Adam Hamilton and Mike Slaughter:
The New Adapters

CONTENTS

INTRODUCTION

There was a time not too long ago when families would sit down together and watch a television show. Really. All in the same room. Folks who inhabited a dwelling and considered themselves a family would watch TV together. There was no such thing as binge-watching or using a DVR. If you wanted to see your favorite show, you had to be at a certain place at a certain time and, yes, usually with certain people.

For decades, often the favorite show portrayed the favorite family. In the 1950s and 60s, many of us chose *Leave It to Beaver*, when we would find out the latest mess Beaver had gotten himself into. If we wanted to learn how Ward Cleaver extricated his son with wisdom and patience, we would be on the couch with Mom and Dad at 7:00 p.m. on Thursday night with the TV tuned to our local ABC affiliate (one of the three stations on our TV). As we watched, there was a feeling that the Cleavers were like us and we were like them.

Family dynamics evolved quickly, it seemed. If the Cleavers were the family of the 50s and 60s, the Bunkers were the family of the 70s. *All in the Family* was without question the favorite TV family of the decade. If you are familiar with both shows and can picture Ward Cleaver and Archie Bunker side by side, then you might wonder, "What in the world happened between the 60s and 70s?" Ward's perfect hair and suit gave way to Archie's sloppy clothes and bombastic temperament. *All in the Family* defied conventions and shattered taboos about the family unit, and many people identified with the Bunkers. People saw their family in that crazy family. These were real people dealing with real issues. People thought, "This is us."

TV families continued to evolve through the '80s, the '90s, and into the twenty-first century: *The Jeffersons, Roseanne, Parenthood, Modern Family,* and the multigenerational, multiethnic show that literally is called *This Is Us.* It appears that the further we move away from Beaver, the closer we come to admitting just how messy our families really are.

If your life often feels messy, imperfect, and dysfunctional, then this book is for you. If your family is anything but typical and sometimes drives you crazy, I have a story to tell you. It is a story for those of us who, even in our mess, still want to be included and connected. It is a story about how the broken and the imperfect find a place of belonging and meaning. That place is God's messy family. You are included. You can be connected. You can bring your imperfection. You can come just as you are. You have a seat at the family table.

I grew up the baby of the family in a time when kids still played outside. When I got home from school I would play in the neighborhood until I heard my mom's voice with a familiar invitation: "Supper's ready." Hearing that call, I would run to the back door with my brother, and we would scramble to put the dishes on the table. Many times, supper was a favorite home-cooked meal; other times it was a bucket of fried chicken or a pizza, as both Mom and Dad worked. It was messy, for sure. But at that table and in that messy family, I knew I could be me. I didn't have to be a tough third-grader; I could be the baby of the family. All I had to do was sit down and eat.

God is inviting you into something that is bigger than you. It's a family. It's connection. It's inclusion. It's messy. It's home. It's not about doing something, so much as it is about knowing who you are and to whom you belong.

You have a seat at the table. I can't wait to tell you all about God's family, your family.

1

The Myth of the Perfect Family

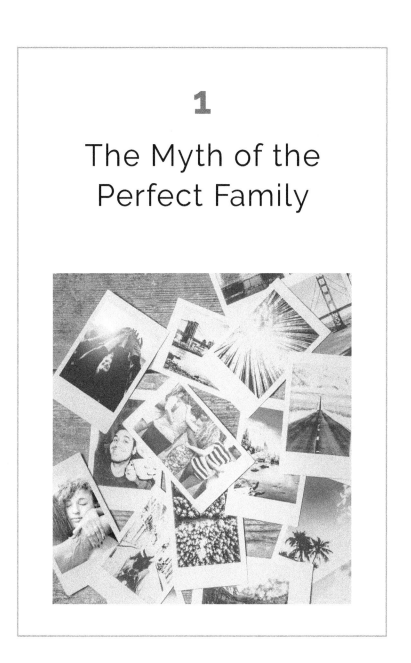

1

THE MYTH OF THE PERFECT FAMILY

My wife and I have a group of people with whom we "do life." We sort of do everything together. I think that is what "doing life" means. We have been part of a small group at our church with these people for nearly ten years. Our kids have grown up together; actually we have all grown up together. Most of us are married, some are single. We have seemingly gone through it all: illnesses, graduations, promotions, demotions. We have experienced life together and, sadly, death together. Just last year we lost one of our beloved group members to cancer. I don't even like to say that we are "like" family. We are family.

Several years ago, when my wife Rachel was pregnant with our third daughter, a couple from our group, Brian and Hollie, told us they were adopting a child. They had just been approved to adopt a son from Ethiopia. We followed their plans closely. We prayed for them and bought them baby gifts. We ate with them at our local Ethiopian restaurant as we dreamed about life with their new son and tried to learn more about his culture.

I remember when they were told his name: Tamirat Yishak. One night at the Ethiopian restaurant they asked the waitress the meaning of Tamirat. She said, "America." Brian and Hollie thought that was strange, a son named America. As they discussed it with the waitress, the restaurant owner came from the kitchen and cleared up the confusion. He said, "No, no, no, you misheard her. His name does not mean 'America'; it means 'a miracle.' " Brian and Hollie decided to keep the name his birth parents had given him: Tamirat Yishak. We call him Ty for short. He is our miracle.

Ty and my daughter Phoebe have grown up together since they were babies. They are both spirited, and they've had many disagreements and more than one argument over a toy. They laugh together. They cry together. They get on each other's nerves. Sometimes they play for hours without even noticing the passage of time.

Ty and Phoebe are family. But when our two families are together—five girls and one boy (sorry, Ty!)—it is . . . well, a mess. We clutter up the kitchen. We spread out toys. We track mud onto the floor. And it's loud, trust me. But it's our messy family, and we love it.

Meet God's Family

Most likely there are parts of your family that are a mess—either your biological family or a family of friends. That's what this book is about, a really messy family. It's about what I would call *the* family in the Bible. A family known as God's family. They are a big, beautiful mess, and the best part is that we've all been adopted into it. It's important you know that. You have been included not in a perfect family, but in a family where your imperfections are known and you are loved anyway. Understanding your place in this family may be the most important thing you ever do.

But before I can tell you about this family—your family—we need to discuss the myth of the perfect family. Somewhere along the way we came up with this idea of a perfect family. They dress just right, they get along fine, and they look nothing like our real family. Maybe the myth took shape for you when, as a child, you visited a friend's family who appeared to have it all together. Maybe they ate around a table every night. Maybe the parents seemed happily married, while your parents fought every night. Maybe you watched a TV show such as *Leave It to Beaver* that seemed to present a family without flaws. But the perfect family is a myth. In fact, the goal of family isn't perfection. It's knowing and being known. It's connection. It's finding your place in a world where often we feel out of place.

Abraham's family (maybe you've heard of them) is pretty much the family in the Bible. Abraham, the father of the family, eventually becomes known as the father of all God's people, Father Abraham. Abraham has a son named Isaac, and Isaac has a son named Jacob. These two sons become so important that in the Bible, God is often referred to as "the God of Abraham, Isaac, and Jacob." Imagine that! Your family becomes known as God's family. They are the most highly revered fathers, and their wives—Sarah, Rebekah, and Rachel—are the most highly revered mothers. In biblical times, every Hebrew family knew those names. When the stories of Abraham's family were told around glowing campfires, it was not unlike our family gatherings around glowing TV sets. Those families, like our families, said, "This is us."

The people of God (the Jews) and the followers of Jesus (the Christians) all say they are part of Father Abraham's family. Muslims, too, trace their lineage to this ancient patriarch. Today almost four billion people are connected to the spiritual family of Abraham. Are they the perfect family? Only if you overlook the first story about Abraham and Sarah, when Abraham lied. Perfect family? Only if you forget that Abraham moved away from his closest family members because they argued too much. You also have to forget that Isaac actually wasn't Abraham's first son; Abraham had a son with another woman while he was still married to Sarah. And Jacob wasn't Isaac's first son either. That was Esau, and Jacob tricked Esau into selling his birthright. Jacob took the birthright from Esau and lied to his father. Jacob's sons, enraged, ended up selling Joseph into slavery. Lying, cheating, arguing—this is us? Of course it is.

God's family, it turns out, is a mess—a big, beautiful mess, but a mess nonetheless. God uses the story of Abraham's family to call us into the family. Sometimes we live in such a way that we think, "I can't be part of the story. I can't keep those promises. I lie. I cheat. I argue. Doesn't God know me?"

God says, "I do know you. My family is your family. And that means that all the promises, all the miracles, all the healing— those are for you too." God has a big, messy family, and you are a part of it.

A Family Trip

Abraham's story started a long time ago. Abraham's dad, Terah, first named his son Abram (not Abraham yet). The name Abram meant "exalted father." We don't know if Terah just liked the sound of the name or if he had a hope that Abram would become a great father. But, as we will see, that name would be important.

Terah had three sons; some even think the sons could have been triplets because of the way their birth is described. The Scripture says, "After Terah had lived 70 years, he became the father of Abram, Nahor and Haran" (Genesis 11:26). There is no way to know if they were triplets, and it isn't important, except that it's fun to imagine they might have had the same family dynamics as Kate, Kevin, and Randall in *This Is Us*. Anyway, Abram, Nahor, and Haran were born to Terah, and later, Haran had a son named Lot. Then Haran died. So Lot tagged along with Terah and Abram and the family. Abram married Sarai (not yet Sarah), whose name meant "my princess." It's not hard for us to imagine a dad naming his daughter "my princess," but all we are told about Sarai is that she was unable to have any kids.

Yeah, I know it's complicated. Hang with me.

Terah (dad/granddad) took Abram (son/husband/uncle) and Sarai (daughter/wife/aunt) and Lot (grandson/nephew) and moved them from Ur, where they had been living, to Canaan. Ur was in present-day Iraq. Canaan was in present-day Israel. The journey would have been about eleven hundred miles on foot. However, about halfway between Ur and Canaan they gave up. They stopped at a place called Harran (not to be confused with Haran, Abraham's brother who died), near what is now the border of Syria and Turkey.

At that point Terah died. And so *the* family, the great family of God's people, stalled out in Harran, where they stayed for years. The group consisted of an older Abram, whose name was "father" but who had no kids; his wife Sarai, a "princess" who was known only for her inability to conceive; and Lot, an orphan who was effectively now their child.

It was in that situation, with those family dynamics, in a place that was not their home, that God came back to Abram and said:

> *"Go from your country, your people and your*
> *father's household to the land I will show you.*
>
> *"I will make you into a great nation,*
> *and I will bless you;*

> *I will make your name great,*
> *and you will be a blessing."*
> *(Genesis 12:1-2)*

And there's more:

> *"I will bless those who bless you,*
> *and whoever curses you I will curse;*
> *and all peoples on earth*
> *will be blessed through you."*
> *(Genesis 12:3)*

In case you aren't catching on, this is crazy! Some random dude who was traveling with his dad to a foreign land, who gave up on the trip years ago because it was too long, was now being told (by God!) that his family would become a great nation that would bless all the people on earth, and that one day billions of people would know his name and trace their lineage to him. God told random Abram to go . . . and he went.

> *Abram was seventy-five years old when he*
> *set out from Harran. He took his wife Sarai,*
> *his nephew Lot, all the possessions they had*
> *accumulated and the people they had acquired*
> *in Harran, and they set out for the land of*
> *Canaan.*
> *(Genesis 12:4-5)*

God's message to Abram had been "Go." A more literal translation might be "Walk." Abram and his messy family walked the remaining five hundred miles. Of course, that's the distance in a straight line on a map; it's farther than that when you travel on mountain passes and desert trails. Imagine walking ten miles a day for a couple of months. Every day you search for water. You defend yourself from other travelers. You endure bad weather. Imagine doing this when you are seventy-five years old.

Keep in mind that this was Abram's second five-hundred-mile trip. The first time, he was a young man filled with hope and adventure, going because his father had asked him to. Now he was an old man who knew how tough the journey would be, who was going because God had told him to. God had called on Abram to take a family trip. And on that trip, Abram became the exalted father of our family.

Notice the way God's invitation was expressed. First came God's actions:

I will make you into a great nation.
I will bless you.
I will make your name great.

Then God described our actions:

You will be a blessing.

God said, I will make you a great nation, I will bless you, and I will make your name great. And *you* will be a blessing.

Keep that in mind.

Normal and Extraordinary

After a long journey, Abram arrived in Canaan at a place known as "the oak of Moreh" (Genesis 12:6 NRSV). In other words, he wasn't showing up in some barren, deserted place. It was inhabited, as you might surmise, by Canaanites. Abram was coming to a place that he believed God had said was for him and his family, but most likely the Canaanites thought it was for them!

Once again, though, God promised Abram, "To your offspring I will give this land" (Genesis 12:7). Abram, whose name meant "father," was told at seventy-five years old that the foreign land he has just entered would be given to his children and grandchildren. One problem: he had no children or grandchildren.

What did Abram do? He got down on his knees and began to gather rocks to make an altar. In my imagination, he was joined by Sarai the princess and Lot the orphan. After a five-hundred-mile trek through the desert, this strange little family built an altar to the God who had spoken to them. This family that looked nothing like *Leave It to Beaver* built an altar and called upon the Lord.

I learn about this family that goes where God wants, that sticks together, that travels through the desert, and I think, "This is us." I read about this family that gathers rocks, that builds an altar to God, that uses the altar to remind each other they are still walking because of their Lord, and I think, "This is us."

The very next episode in the family story has Abram lying to a king, saying that Sarai is his sister and not his wife. He lies to protect his own skin and to get a few cows. In the next episode, Abram and Lot part ways, because there is too much arguing among their respective parties. The people who work for Abram and the people who work for Lot can't get along, and instead of Abram and Lot working it out, they walk away.

I read about this family that lies and cheats, that is afraid, that is made up of individuals looking out for their own gain, and I think that sounds familiar. I hear of this family that argues, that is unwilling to work it out and work it through, that is frail and fragile and not as strong as we would like, and I think, "This is us."

So which is it? Was Abram's family ordinary—prone to wander, to fight and flee, to be given a good name but be unable to live up to it? Or were they extraordinary—chosen, living into their calling, giving God glory? Was Abram a normal dad, or was he the exalted father?

The answer is the same answer that applies to your family and family members. They were normal; they were great. They were ordinary; they were extraordinary. Abram was like your dad; Abram walked with God.

And the whole world was blessed through Abram and Sarai and their family.

Becoming a Blessing

How does God's family become a blessing?
We build altars.
We call upon the name of the Lord.
We live into our names over time.

I walked two miles with my family of five the other day. When we were done I felt like building an altar and praising God! We stopped fifty times. We had to carry some people. We had to coax and encourage.

Abram walked five hundred miles with his family, and when he was done he built an altar of praise. It was an altar of "Thank you, God," of "God, you did what you said you would do." That was Abram's first altar, an altar of praise.

When they arrived, they pitched their tent. This would be their home. And there, where he would see it every day coming out of the tent, Abram built a second altar. This was an altar of prayer, a place where the family would talk to God day after day after day, not just when God did big stuff. This imperfect family called upon the name of the Lord every day.

I don't want to simplify this too much, but if you're looking for meaning and for a place in God's family, then build an altar of praise and an altar of prayer. Find a place where you remember and thank God for who God is and also a place where you call out to God. Build an altar of praise and an altar of prayer. Call upon the name of the Lord in your messy, broken life. Abram called out to God after he lied and before he parted ways with Lot. Abram wasn't perfect, but he had an altar. We must call upon the Lord in the big times and the normal times.

It was then, on arriving at their destination, that Abram and Sarai began to live into the names God would give them: "father" and "princess." God kept telling them he was going to bless them and use them to bless others. They lived into that promise; they literally walked into that promise over time.

This is us. This is what a big, messy family looks like, and you are a part of it. It's not perfect, far from it. But we keep walking toward perfection. We keep walking toward the land where God will use our lives to bless others. God told Abram and Sarai that their names would be great and that all the people on earth would be blessed through them. Would we be bold enough to believe that? Would we ask God to make our names great so that others could be blessed?

Some weeks ago Ty's mom, Hollie, came to my office at the church. She had tears in her eyes as she shared her vision for a ministry that would serve parents who are looking to adopt children. She said she wanted to hold an adoption conference at our church. At first I was afraid. I pictured an adoption conference as an event where people would be handing out babies or something. Hollie cleared it up. No, instead it would be an event where those who are thinking about adoption, those who are adopting, and those who already have adopted could find community and support. Hollie shared a dream of children being adopted from all over the world, based on what God has done in their family through Ty. We have begun to dream about what our community would be like with people of all colors and tribes living and serving together. This is us.

I told you that Ty's first name, Tamirat, means "a miracle." Ty's middle name, Yishak—well, you may already have figured that one out. Yishak is simply the Ethiopian name for Isaac. In other words, Ty already carries with him the name of his true family. It's a messy family for sure, but many people have been blessed through it, and I have a sneaking suspicion that many people will be blessed through the little boy who came into our family. Tamirat Yishak—our miracle. God's miracle.

What would it be like if all of us could recognize and accept the blessings in our names? Our broken, messed up, lying, cheating, arguing-so-much-I-don't-even-want-to-live-close-to-my-family names? We can be normal and also be great. We can be a family that builds altars. We can be a messy family that calls upon the name of the Lord.

Maybe you have a great earthly family, or maybe you've never felt that you belonged in a family. God is inviting us and adopting us into a great, normal, messy family, the family of God.

2

The Gap Between What God Says and What You See

2

THE GAP BETWEEN
WHAT GOD SAYS
AND WHAT YOU SEE

Driving my kids to school one morning recently I was reminded of something. A day can feel really long. In the car line at school, my youngest daughter, Phoebe, asked me how many hours are in the school day. I could see her pondering how long a day feels, like she ages a year each day at school.

I added it up in my head. "Seven. Seven hours in the school day."

Phoebe said, "Seeevveen!?"

"Yep, seven."

"Why do they make us go seven?" she asked, exasperated.

"I don't know, Phoebe. I don't know."

Keep in mind this is the same child who, during first grade, said as we pulled up to school each morning, "Welcome to the torture chamber." After watching the movie *The Princess Bride*, she has more recently modified that to say, "Welcome to the pit of despair," which I think is a bit more descriptive. I'm proud she is expanding her vocabulary.

When you are arriving at school in second grade, the day just stretches out before you, and if you are Phoebe, you are seriously wondering if you will live long enough to make it to the dismissal bell at the end of the school day.

Life feels that way sometimes. The week can seem really long when you get up on Monday morning. College is daunting when you arrive as a freshman on campus. When you began your career, you might have felt excited about the future, but now, some years in, you may be wondering, "How long is this going to last?"

In my neck of the woods everybody posts pictures on social media the first day of school. The most common picture is one of a child on the front porch, backpack on, holding a simple placard that says "First day of kindergarten" or "First day of third grade" or another appropriate dating of that historic moment. Last fall my neighbor, the dad of the family, had his picture taken on the front porch. He held a placard that said "4085th day of work."

In the Gap

The school day has a gap between morning and afternoon. Phoebe knows she has to get through the day to make it back home to her family—seven hours; she can do this. But what about those of us who pour the cup of coffee and head off to work? Where are we going? When does this end? Is life just something to be endured? Are we counting the days to retirement? It can sure seem that way sometimes. We should feel purpose in our daily lives, in our daily tasks, in where we are; but most of us would be lying if we didn't say that sometimes we're in the gap. And we really don't know where it ends.

The hit TV show *This Is Us* has been compelling to so many, I think, because it has a big gap that we can't see. What I mean is it shows a young couple raising their three kids and all the craziness of that, and it also shows us thirty years later with the kids grown and the craziness of that. But the gap in between is mostly unknown to us. What we learn in watching the show each week is that the things that happened in the gap are the most important. We realize that for us to understand where the characters in the show are now and where they are going, we have to know more about what happened during the in between, in the gap.

Abram and his family were the *This Is Us* of the ancient world. We know the beginning and ending of their story, when God's promises were first made and finally fulfilled. Thankfully, we also know the in-between. We might be tempted to skip over it, but if we do, we miss the most important parts for understanding our own stories and families.

When Abram and Sarai arrived in Canaan, they had spent the course of their adult lives on a journey. The journey must have seemed haphazard at times, and they must have been tempted to give up. Their arrival in Canaan ended an eleven-hundred-mile trek on foot. In Canaan, God renewed the crazy promise that not only would he bless Abram; he would give Abram and Sarai as many offspring as stars in the sky.

God said, "Abram, I give this land to you and your offspring."

To which Abram may have said, "Great, but I ain't got no offspring!" And yet, Abram built an altar to say, "I believe."

God kept promising and Abram kept waiting. In Genesis 15 there is a captivating conversation between Abram and God that we cannot overlook. In it, we see Abram's struggle with the wait and his doubt regarding the promises.

> *Abram said, "Sovereign LORD, what can you*
> *give me since I remain childless and the one who*
> *will inherit my estate is Eliezer of Damascus?"*
> *And Abram said, "You have given me no*
> *children; so a servant in my household will be*
> *my heir."*
> (Genesis 15:2-3)

It's as if Abram was saying, "I love all these promises, God, I really do. But I've been waiting so long, and I just want to point out a few things. My name is Abram, which means 'exalted father.' But eleven hundred miles and several decades back, I've known we couldn't have children. And five hundred miles back, you told me I would be a great nation. Now I'm in my eighties, and here you are still promising. I want to believe, but if I die today, Eliezer—some guy we picked up along the way—would inherit everything I have. Nothing against Eliezer, he's a good guy, but don't you see how your promises are not fitting with the reality of my life? God, what you're saying and what I'm seeing are two totally different things."

Obviously, I'm putting words into Abram's mouth, but it's not hard to imagine he might have had these feelings. Abram was saying: There is a gap here.

Abram Believed

There is a gap here.

How many of us feel that way? How many of us go to church week after week and hear a pastor talking about promises? We hear promises about healing, about the riches of knowing and being close to God, about good things to come, about hope and beauty and restoration. Do you ever sit there and think, "I don't want to be rude, Pastor. I actually like hearing it, but there seems to be a gap between what you're saying and what I'm seeing."

Well, that's Abram's story. That's our family story. God told Abram he was going to have so many stinking kids it wasn't even funny. And Abram thought, "That's awesome, God, but I'm eighty-four years old and don't have one kid."

That's when God took Abram outside (it seems they had been in Abram's tent), and God said,

> "Look up at the sky and count the stars—if
> indeed you can count them." Then he said to
> him, "So shall your offspring be."
>
> *(Genesis 15:5)*

And what did Abram do? Abram believed.

He could have rolled his eyes; he could have thought, "Okay whatever," and maybe he did some of that. But the Scripture says that when Abram found himself in the gap, he believed.

Abram and God continued talking for a bit, and then Abram fell asleep, and "a thick and dreadful darkness came over him" (Genesis 15:12). Did you catch that? In the gap—the time between the promise being made and the promise being fulfilled—Abram experienced darkness.

Maybe it was a little bit like Phoebe at school. I know seven hours isn't that long. I know Phoebe can make it through the day. But try telling that to a second-grader who sees school as the pit of despair. It's a long time!

God saw the endgame for Abram. God knew the promise would come true. Abram wanted to believe, but it must have seemed so long to him.

About That Gap

Many of us are in a gap right now, between what God says and what we see. Here are a few things to keep in mind.

The gap can be really dark.

Reading about the darkness, perhaps it would be going too far to say that Abram suffered from depression. But I think it's possible, and I know that faithful followers of Jesus, when in the gap, can experience thick and dreadful darkness. They may experience depression, and my guess is Abram suffered from it at some point in the decades while he waited for God's promise to come true.

The gap can be really long.

Spoiler alert, but Abram and Sarai remained childless until Abram was ninety-nine years old. That was a really long time to wait after being told, decades before, that he would father a great nation. If right now you're experiencing a very long gap between what God says and what you see, remember Abram.

The gap can feel really messy.

Abram's family story is really messy. It gets messier. The next story in the Bible tells us that Abram, after waiting nine more years for children, has a child with Sarai's servant Hagar. This was not what God had promised. So, now Abram had a child with another woman. Sarai, who was in on the plan of using Hagar to fulfill God's promise, ended up getting jealous. She sent Hagar and the child, Ishmael, out into the wilderness. Now, that's messy. There were lots of emotions, a bunch of mistakes, and people's lives were involved. If your family has cancer or divorce or rebellious teenagers or other things that make life and families messy, then pay attention.

Learning Patience

If you are like me, you might find that you are growing more and more impatient. And if the roadways are any indication, others are growing impatient too! Much of my impatience comes with having a full plate, a full schedule, and an inflated sense of my own importance. So when one little thing goes wrong, everything goes wrong, and my day becomes a mess.

I might (hypothetically) stand in the ten-item express lane at the grocery store and look at the guy in front of me who clearly has seventeen items (I counted them) and begin to wish destruction on his life. I might even begin to think negative thoughts about the teenage clerk who should be upholding the sacred ten-item rule. Suddenly I feel anger and disdain toward other humans because my wife asked me to pick up cornstarch at the grocery store and I don't even know what cornstarch is. It's hard to find something when you don't know what it is, and it really does sound like something that might be shelved with the laundry detergent. I thought starch was for shirts, not food, and so it's embarrassing when I ask someone in the laundry detergent aisle if they know where the cornstarch is, and they don't even say anything, they just look at me. But I did find the cornstarch because I Googled it, and now here I stand behind Mr. Seventeen Items in the Ten-Item Express Lane, and the checkout guy isn't doing anything about it. And I'm impatient! Which is interesting because God is patient. What we see in Abram's story is that God is very, very patient.

If we are to learn patience in our lives and with our families, we have to understand that God's idea of time is different from ours. That can be annoying, sure, but it is for real. There's a line in the Bible where Peter says, "Do not forget this one thing" (2 Peter 3:8). I think we should be interested in what Peter says is the one thing we should not forget. Peter was about as close to Jesus as anyone was, and so I think we should wonder what that one thing is. Ready?

Here, in that same verse, is Peter's one thing: "With the Lord a day is like a thousand years, and a thousand years are like a day."

For us a day is twenty-four hours—fifteen, sixteen, seventeen hours awake and the rest asleep. For us a day is a very limited thing; we only get so many of them. But for God a day is like a thousand years, and a thousand years are like a day. God looks at, conceives of, and experiences time differently than we do. Abram was in time, and we are in time—God's time. To understand God's patience, we must remember that God's time is different.

Peter extends this insight in the next verse: "The Lord is not slow in keeping his promise, as some understand slowness" (2 Peter 3:9). Sometimes we think God is slow, but the Lord is not slow in keeping promises. God simply looks at slowness differently than we do.

A Different Pace

My express lane story could have been told twenty years ago. That's about how long grocery stores have had express lanes. These days, we are not an express-lane society. Groceries can be ordered online and delivered to your car or your house. We are a long way from the neighborhood markets of my grandparents' generation, where you knew the owner of the market and bought things on credit. The supermarket sped things up and further separated us from people, which led to the express lane and then self-checkout and now groceries being delivered to your front door. I use this one arena as an example of how our world has sped up, making us less relational and more impatient. I'm not against more efficient and expedient ways of getting groceries; I'm just saying that surely we can see how God might have a different idea about slowness than we do!

It's really important that we pause in Abram's story and try to understand God's patience, because it affects how we understand God's promises. The Lord is not slow in keeping promises; the Lord is simply walking at a different pace. To which we say, "God, keep up!" To which God might say, "No, you slow down." As we find God's pace, we begin to see more of God's promises. In fact, God's apparent delays are all about keeping promises.

It's in the delay or the gap that we most often are tempted to take matters into our own hands. It's in the mess that we try to clean up by ourselves. Abram and Sarai took matters into their own hands when they decided to have a child through Hagar. Then they tried to clean up the mess by sending Hagar away. That just made more of a mess, and the more they took matters into their own hands, the messier it got.

Our family story teaches us that in the gap time we are not supposed to speed things up or push to make God's promises happen. If you are in darkness, don't give up. If you are depressed, don't give up. Abram knew thick and dreadful darkness, but he didn't give up on the promise. God promises light and love and blessing. It is coming.

In the meantime, I believe in the biblical principle of *hang in there*. I see it in Abram and Sarai. I see it in Joseph, whom we will look at later. I see it in Ruth and Esther. I see it in Mary Magdalene. I see it in Peter. I see it in the cross and in the grave that Jesus walked out of. Hang the heck in there.

Abram and Sarai teach us that the meantime is most of the time, when we hang in and hold out hope in the gap between what God says and what we can see.

Sweep Faithfully

My first job, at age sixteen, was at a feed store. I would carry sacks of feed to people's pickup trucks. If it was one or two sacks I could throw them over my shoulder; for more than that I needed a dolly to roll them outside.

One of my first days on the job, the owner of the store explained that if I was not carrying sacks of feed, I was to be sweeping. He pointed me to an old push broom leaning against the back wall. The store had a huge concrete floor, and it was a feed store, so the floor was often covered in bits of corn and grain. I asked him where I should sweep it all, since there wasn't even a dustpan. He said he didn't care where I swept it; he just wanted me sweeping.

So I got started. I found that I was an impatient sweeper. It seemed like a waste of time. I didn't understand the purpose. But I kept sweeping.

In short time I was given other jobs. I was asked to throw bales of hay off a big stack and onto trailers. Pretty soon I was trained to fill propane tanks. I was nearing the top of the food chain. By this time there had been other folks hired who did the more menial jobs I had started with. I mean, I was propane man. This was about as good as it gets. But after some months on the job, I was surprised by something. When I wasn't filling propane tanks or throwing bales of hay or carrying sacks of feed, I went back to sweeping. What the owner taught me as a young man was that there will be fleeting moments of glory, when you fill propane tanks. There will be adventuresome times, when you hurl hay stacks. But most of the time is sweeping time, and the person you are when sweeping at the back of the store is the person you will be when greater opportunities come. So, sweep faithfully.

Our Spiritual Heritage

Abram's years of waiting steeled in him a patience and a belief that would be evident when the promises were fulfilled. The in-between time is not without meaning, and we shouldn't wish away the meantime. The meantime is most of the time. Abram's family learned, during those messy in-between times, that God is at work.

This is our spiritual heritage. This is our family story. We believe God is working in the midst of our messes. That's really what the Bible is about: belief. Belief is our heritage. It is what Abram passed down to us, and it's what we are to pass down to our kids in the same way that our parents passed things down to us.

My parents passed down to me a love of music, an affinity for the mountains, and silver hair at a young age. Your parents may have given you a mechanical mind or a strong sense of family. Your grandfather may have passed down the desire to fish or to serve your country. Some of us have a tendency toward addiction or running away or yelling too much. We all have a heritage. Your spiritual heritage, passed down through Father Abraham, is belief. Hanging in there, holding out hope, and believing God is at work even when you can't see it.

Paul wrote in depth about Abraham and the spiritual heritage that he passed down to us. Here are some of the insights Paul offered in Romans 4:13, 16, 19-21.

> *It was not through the law that Abraham and his offspring received the promise that he would be heir of the world, but through the righteousness that comes by faith.* [What did Abraham do? He believed!]

> *Therefore, the promise comes by faith, so that it may be by grace and may be guaranteed to all Abraham's offspring—not only to those who are of the law but also to those who have the faith of Abraham. He is the father of us all.* [The promise comes through belief and is guaranteed to Abraham's offspring. That's us! Abraham is the father of us all.]

*Without weakening in his faith, he faced the fact
that his body was as good as dead—since he was
about a hundred years old—and that Sarah's
womb was also dead. Yet he did not waver
through unbelief regarding the promise of God,
but was strengthened in his faith and gave glory
to God, being fully persuaded that God had
power to do what he had promised.* [Promises
are delivered in the unlikeliest of vessels. God
keeps promises.]

My girls are growing up, but when I look at them, I still see
my children. They are stressed about school. And I'm like, "Let's
go outside and look at the stars. Can you count the stars?"

We may be in the gap, the in-between time, but to God we
are right where we need to be. God looks at old man Abraham
and thinks, "I can't wait to fulfill these great promises in you."

God has promises for you, too.

3

No, Nothing Is Too Hard for the Lord

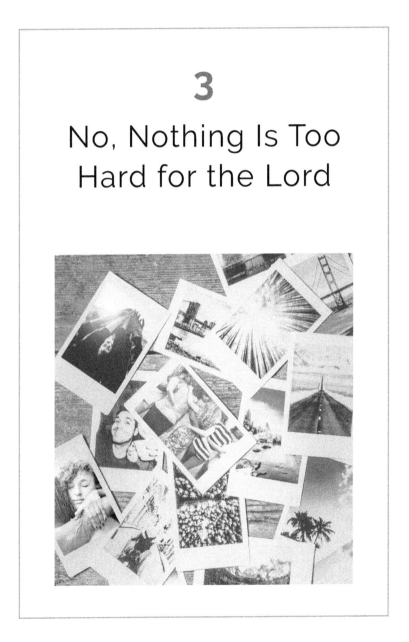

3

NO, NOTHING IS TOO HARD FOR THE LORD

The Lord kept appearing in Abraham's life. No matter where he went, no matter what was going on, the Lord kept showing up. I don't know if you feel that way too. No matter where you go, no matter what happens in your life, God keeps appearing.

Anyway, one day when Abraham was ninety-nine years old, the Lord appeared yet again. Abraham was living in a tent in a land that God said would be given to Abraham and his offspring. (He still had no offspring.) That day, he was doing what people who live in arid, desert climates do during the heat of the day: sitting in the shade.

What was Abraham thinking about? Was he napping?

We can't be sure, but we do know that just a few days before, God had given him a new name. Some of you noticed it. His name had been Abram (which means "exalted father"). Everywhere Abram had gone, he had been greeted, "Hey, Exalted Father!" Which was embarrassing, because he still had no kids.

Now, at the ripe old age of ninety-nine, God was giving him a new name. One might think he would be happy to get a new name. Finally he could shed this Exalted Father moniker. And what was Abram's new name? It was Abraham, which means "father of many nations." Probably not the upgrade he was looking for. Can you imagine how it went when he told his friends?

"Um, I have a new name, guys. My name is now Abraham. I realize I still don't have any kids, but if you could call me Father of Many Nations, that would be great."

By the way, Sarai got a new name too. It was Sarah, which means (you guessed it) "mother of many nations."

What the Strangers Said

So, when Abraham was sitting outside his tent that hot day, maybe he was thinking about his new name. Maybe he was pondering the gap between what God had promised and what had been delivered. That's when the Lord appeared.

> *Abraham looked up and saw three men standing*
> *nearby. When he saw them, he hurried from the*
> *entrance of his tent to meet them and bowed low*
> *to the ground.*
>
> (Genesis 18:2)

Abraham, living in a culture where hospitality for the stranger was valued, bowed to the men. This was a bit different from our culture. When someone shows up at our house, we hide and hope they will leave the package on the front stoop. If there's no package involved, we expect people to text before they stop by. But Abraham ran out and bowed.

> He said, "If I have found favor in your eyes, my lord, do not pass your servant by. Let a little water be brought, and then you may all wash your feet and rest under this tree. Let me get you something to eat, so you can be refreshed and then go on your way—now that you have come to your servant."
>
> (verses 3-5)

Abraham had just set in motion an unplanned, extravagant banquet. He told Sarah to bake some bread. He brought milk and curds. He had a servant select a choice calf. In other words, Abraham gave his best to the strangers. We wonder: Did Abraham realize that God was visiting him? Did he do the same for all strangers? We don't know yet.

One of the strangers said, "I will surely return to you about this time next year, and Sarah your wife will have a son" (verse 10).

How did Abraham respond? Other than, "Huh? What did you say?"

My guess is that Abram, now Abraham, remembered some earlier encounters with God. Rewind twenty-four years, when Abram woke up in another tent five hundred miles away and God said Abram's family would be a great nation. Rewind to his arrival in Canaan, when God said the land would belong to Abram's offspring, and he built an altar. Rewind a few years earlier, when Abram called God's bluff and said, in effect, "If I die today, my servant gets everything." So God took Abraham outside and asked him to count the stars, saying, "That's how big your legacy will be."

Sarah Laughed

During Abraham's conversation with the three strangers, Sarah had been listening from behind the tent flap. When she heard the stranger promise a baby boy, she threw back her head and laughed. Well, the Bible says she laughed to herself, so maybe she covered her mouth and had a good private chuckle.

> Then the LORD said to Abraham, "Why did
> Sarah laugh and say, 'Will I really have a child,
> now that I am old?' "
>
> *(Genesis 18:13)*

Wait, time out. "The LORD said to Abraham"? I'm guessing this is how they wrote it down later, because suddenly the three strangers had become God. And God said,

"Is anything too hard for the LORD? I will return
to you at the appointed time next year, and
Sarah will have a son."

(verse 14)

Sarah heard this promise. God asked why she had laughed, and in one of the best lines in all of Scripture, Sarah said, "I did not laugh." And God said, "Yes, you did" (verse 15).

Fast-forward one year, and guess what? Sarah had a baby boy! It's worth reading the whole baby announcement:

Now the LORD was gracious to Sarah as he had
said, and the LORD did for Sarah what he had
promised. Sarah became pregnant and bore a
son to Abraham in his old age, at the very time
God had promised him. Abraham gave the
name Isaac to the son Sarah bore him. When
his son Isaac was eight days old, Abraham
circumcised him, as God commanded him.
Abraham was a hundred years old when his son
Isaac was born to him.

Sarah said, "God has brought me laughter, and
everyone who hears about this will laugh with
me." And she added, "Who would have said to
Abraham that Sarah would nurse children? Yet I
have borne him a son in his old age."

(Genesis 21:1-7)

Guys, this is an ancient story. It has been told around campfires and family tables. It has been recounted in mansions and cathedrals. But this is our story. This is our family. This is us.

What to Do When God Shows Up

Our family story seems to say that when we welcome the stranger, we welcome God. Without a doubt, one of the coolest Scriptures in the whole Bible is where it says, "Do not neglect to show hospitality to strangers, for thereby some have entertained angels unawares" (Hebrews 13:2 ESV). We have spent time in the presence of God when we have spent time caring for people we don't know.

When God shows up, we need to be ready to throw a banquet. We need to live ready to give our best, ready to pour it out. How do we know when God shows up? The story of Abraham teaches that at first you usually don't know! And so we are to treat all people the way we would act if God were a guest in our home. If we need to clarify what kind of people, Jesus says the least people, the people who need food, drink, clothes, and shelter.

Abraham threw an extravagant party when three strangers showed up at his house, and in so doing he got to party with God. God's messy family welcomes others in and treats strangers like family, because it turns out they are family.

Jesus caught flak from religious folks when he preached this message. In response to criticism about welcoming and even eating with outsiders, Jesus told a story about a lost sheep. Jesus said, "Suppose one of you has a hundred sheep and loses one of them. Doesn't he leave the ninety-nine in the open country and go after the lost sheep until he finds it?" (Luke 15:4). If you are like me and have heard the parable of the lost sheep a bunch of times, you may nod along with Jesus' question and say, "Yes, Jesus, a shepherd would leave the ninety-nine to go after the one." But those listening to his original telling of the story, a people more familiar with sheep and shepherding than I am, may well have said, "No! What kind of shepherd would leave ninety-nine to go after one wayward sheep?" Maybe in fact Jesus' story should be called the parable of the crazy shepherd, and we're the ones who are supposed to be crazy. Jesus ends the story by saying,

> *"When he finds it, he joyfully puts it on his shoulders and goes home. Then he calls his friends and neighbors together and says, 'Rejoice with me; I have found my lost sheep.' I tell you that in the same way there will be more rejoicing in heaven over one sinner who repents than over ninety-nine righteous persons who do not need to repent."*
>
> *(Luke 15:5-7)*

Jesus follows this story with the parable of the lost coin, about a lady who wakes people in the middle of the night to celebrate finding a coin; and the prodigal son, the story of a father who selects the choice calf to have a party for his rascal son coming home. Apparently those of us in God's family need to be prepared to throw more parties. We should be looking for God in the stranger, in the least, and in the lost. We need to risk the banquet, in hopes that we might spend time in the presence of God.

When I think about a shepherd partying over a sheep or a lady over a coin, I have to smile and maybe even laugh. It's okay, though. Our family story says it's fine to let out a laugh in the face of the crazy things God is doing. After all, Sarah laughed and they named their son Isaac, which means "he laughs."

It's okay to laugh with God along the journey. It's okay to be so amazed by God that you chuckle. God is so extravagant with his promises that you may think to yourself that it's crazy. But it's not laughing at God; it's laughing with God. It's embracing joy. It's naming your kid He Laughs. God gives us such a good story, such an outrageous promise, such a crazy, messed-up family that we have to laugh.

Learning from Lukas

My friend Lukas, a member of our church and a part of God's family, has taught me many things. In the hours after Lukas was born, he suffered a massive stroke that paralyzed his entire right side. It was five days before he was stable enough for doctors to run the necessary tests to determine what had happened, and once they knew, the prognosis was not good. Mike and Jenn, his parents, remember standing in a hospital hallway as a doctor told them Lukas would likely never walk or talk and would have significant impairments. They prayed that God would heal him. Lukas's mom Jenn says of that prayer and of their experience in the years since:

> I admit that the healing I prayed for in those first horrible days is not what we have seen. I wanted that instant, lightning bolt kind of change. But what we have received over these past twelve years is more like a gentle rain, steady, restorative, and sometimes messy.[1]

A couple of years later Lukas had another setback. Seizures began to escalate and couldn't be controlled by medicines. Lukas had major brain surgery. He spent weeks in the hospital and was released just days before Easter.

After the surgery Lukas started to talk. He began to scoot around the floor. When he was almost four years old, he pulled himself up to stand on Christmas morning. Lukas is now known for his remarkable spirit. He has an astounding capacity to love and empathize. He laughs, a lot. He exudes joy.

When Lukas was four years old and barely walking, he got away from Jenn and Mike at a friend's wedding. It took a few minutes for Jenn to find him, and when she did, he was leaning against a woman she didn't know. His one good arm was wrapped around the woman, and his head rested on her shoulder. Tears streamed down the woman's face. Jenn didn't know what to say. Finally the woman told her, "I was just sitting here feeling

---

1 Jennifer Rodia, "God Surprises Us," RethinkChurch.org, United Methodist Communications, accessed May 2, 2018, http://www.rethinkchurch.org/articles/easter/god-surprises-us.

completely alone in this crowded room, when this child came out of nowhere and took my hand and hugged me."

There are a bunch of Lukas stories like that, stories that makes us say, "Nothing is too hard for the Lord."

A couple of years ago, Lukas didn't want to go church anymore. In a variety of ways, subtle and not so subtle, he let it be known that he wasn't interested in going. Finally, one morning before church, his parents asked in desperation, "Why, Lukas? Why don't you want to go?"

He replied, "I don't want to wear a handsome shirt."

"A handsome shirt?" they asked.

It turned out that Lukas was referring to a button-up shirt, the kind you tuck in. When they found out, they said, "Oh Lukas, this is about a shirt? You can wear whatever shirt you want."

He said, "I want to wear my Star Wars shirt."

When I saw Lukas that Sunday morning, I complimented him on his shirt, further confirming that his mom had been crazy to make him wear a handsome shirt. Then I realized something. I undid my handsome shirt a few buttons and showed him the shirt I was wearing beneath it: Star Wars! Lukas was amazed. His mom and dad were amazed. I had no idea how it had happened, but we all laughed anyway, grateful that our God had a sense of humor.

A Total Eclipse

If the spiritual heritage of Abraham is faith, then the spiritual heritage of Sarah is hearing the question "Is anything too hard for the Lord?" and answering with a resounding "No!"

Abraham and Sarah's family, our family, believes that God can do anything. God can make a boy feel welcomed at church because the pastor wears a Star Wars shirt. God can even make stars come out in the middle of the day. Yeah, you read that right. Remember when God took Abram outside the tent to count the stars? Turns out that it wasn't nighttime. We learn this when, later in that same conversation, we are told that the sun went down. That means when Abram was invited to count the stars, the sun was still out.

I was in middle school—say, 1993—the first time I heard the song "Total Eclipse of the Heart." It had been blasting over FM frequencies and in roller skating rinks for a decade, but somehow I had missed it. When I finally noticed it, I was in the school auditorium during the STARS presentation. Acronyms were used a lot back in those days with teenagers. An acronym could make anything cool. STARS (as I'm sure you're dying to know) was an acronym for a campus group called Students Taking a Right Stand. The group spoke out against the use of alcohol, drugs, crude language, and other bad stuff.

That day, I watched as some of my peers walked out onto the darkened stage wearing black T-shirts with white lettering emblazoned on the front. Each shirt had a different bad thing written on it. Heroin. Cocaine. LSD. I don't know how many of my classmates in that small town were snorting coke, but the message was clear. These things were bad, and we should turn away from them.

That's when I heard "Total Eclipse of the Heart," sung by Bonnie Tyler. This moving rock ballad included the repeated phrase "Turn around." At school that day, each time Bonnie Tyler sang "Turn around," the student wearing the Heroin or Cocaine or LSD T-shirt would turn around to show another word on the back of their shirt: like Hope or Promise or Love. I thought it was very cool.

Hold that thought. Now let's go back to Abram.

Already in our short study of God's family, we have spent more time looking at Abram than at Abraham. Abram lived a long, long time in the gap between what God promised and what Abram saw. He was told for years there would be beautiful promises fulfilled, but he saw no evidence of it. Still, he had faith. He was trying to hang in there.

Hanging in there is one kind of faith; being asked to count stars during the day is a different kind of faith altogether. It's laughable. It's crazy and extravagant in the face of circumstances telling you the opposite.

And still Abram believed.

My brother works as a physical scientist for the National Park Service and was in town visiting in 2017. He told me how he was going to drive a considerable distance from his home to the Teton mountains to witness the full totality of the solar eclipse that year. Because my brother knows a lot more about astronomy than I do, I asked him questions about this marvel that would be coming right through my hometown in a few days. He told me several amazing things we could expect, and then he said, "You know, it's quite common during a total solar eclipse for the sky to go completely dark and the stars to come out in the middle of the day."

"Say that again," I said.

He repeated that during a total solar eclipse, the stars can come out in the middle of the day. Now, my brother studies the heavens in one way, and I study them in another. I told him about Abram and the strange story in which God asked him to count stars during the day. Could it have been a solar eclipse? He explained that there are computer-generated forecasts into both the future and the past, telling when and where solar eclipses happen. You know that I Googled it.

According to one source, there was a total solar eclipse in Canaan on May 9, 1533 BC, which appeared to be the very time when a foreigner named Abram had pitched his tent in that place. I'm not saying definitively that the story in Genesis 15 happened on that precise date; I'm just saying we have a God who can cause stars to come out in the middle of the day. I believe that.

Today, those of us who belong to the family of Abraham should lift our gaze upward. Many of us are in a time that could be described as a gap between what God has promised and what we can see. But we are a people who believe that God can turn things around. The turn can be drastic as seeing Heroin one moment and Hope the next. It can be as dramatic as going from LSD to Love in the blink of an eye.

We believe that nothing is too difficult for the Lord. Why? Our family believes God can make stars come out in the middle of the day. Please, people of God, don't stop laughing at the wonders that God works, big and small. After all, this is us. Abram and Sarai. Abraham and Sarah. When God shows up, be ready to throw a party. Even if you're still waiting for promises to come true, laugh and find joy in the messy family to which you belong.

Ask yourself, "Is anything too hard for the Lord?" And answer, along with Sarah and God's great family, "No! Nothing is too hard for the Lord."

4

Loss and Promise
in the Family of God

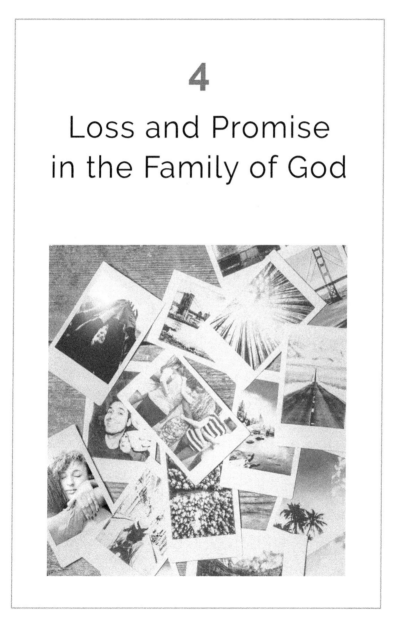

4

LOSS AND PROMISE
IN THE FAMILY OF GOD

Charles and Susan celebrated fifty years of marriage. I was
there. I didn't know them well, but a couple of weeks previous
Susan had introduced herself and asked me if I would stand with
them as they renewed their vows. I said yes.

It was not a formal event. It took place immediately after our
last worship service on a Sunday morning. We stood over in the
corner of our sanctuary. Their daughter was there, along with a
nephew and his children. People were still filing out of the room.
Musicians were on the stage taking down their equipment. Holy
Communion was being cleaned up. Kids were running down the
aisles.

It was a little messy.

Looking over the mess, I asked them, "Is this okay?" After all, the occasion was a solemn one. Fifty years is a long time. They both smiled and said, "Yes, it's fine." I asked them to stand just the way they did fifty years before. They did, and Charles looked as if he had just walked Susan down the aisle.

I said, "Friends, we are gathered here together in the sight of God to witness (again) and bless (again) the marriage of Charles and Susan. The covenant of marriage was established by God…" and off I went. Right there in the mess, the old words of an old promise. Will you love him, comfort him, honor and keep him? The whole deal.

Then I had them face each other, which is what you do during the vows. The bride and groom hand off their flowers and join hands. When Charles looked into Susan's eyes, he began to cry. They repeated the vows after me. Through tears and smiles and with an intensity I guess you can only get after fifty years of going through things together, Charles and Susan promised again. To have and to hold, from this day forward, for better, for worse; for richer, for poorer; in sickness and in health.

I'm convinced that hearts don't age that much, or at least not at the same rate as our bodies or minds. The heart of man or woman in their seventies is a lot like the heart of a man or woman in their twenties. And I can attest that the heart of a thirty-seven-year-old is not much different from the heart of a seventeen-year-old. A heart can get hardened, burdened, wounded. But it doesn't age that much.

What I'm saying is that I didn't actually know Charles and Susan all that well. I can assure you, though, that they had experienced many losses in fifty years. And yet, there they stood with hearts full of promise. In a room filled with messy family, through the fatigue of preaching three services and two funerals the day before, the power of the promise took my breath away.

The Death of Sarah

If you've lived a normal life with normal relationships in a normal family, then you know something of promise and something of loss. Unless you are completely out of the ordinary, you know as much about promises broken as promises kept. Of course, fifty years of marriage is the exception, not the rule. Death and divorce are far more common than the golden anniversary. Most of us have experienced loss. Some of us are experiencing loss in our life right now—loss of a loved one, of a marriage, of a child living at home, of a job.

Even with all that loss, though, most of us are not ready to give up on promising. There's something about our young hearts that still wants to promise.

With that in mind, Genesis 23 can really be given only one title, one heading, one summarizing phrase. It is this: The Death of Sarah. I know we're reading an old, old story, but it's almost hard to read the phrase, isn't it? We've accepted Abraham and Sarah as father and mother to us. They feel like family.

Sarah lived to be a hundred and twenty-seven years old. She died at Kiriath Arba (that is,

Hebron) in the land of Canaan, and Abraham
went to mourn for Sarah and to weep over her.
(Genesis 23:1-2)

We want to be quiet for a moment as we picture Abraham weeping over the loss of his Sarah. They did it. They made the journey. They made it together. They walked from Ur to Harran, 550 miles, based on nothing but a promise. They believed at the age of seventy-five that God would make them a great nation. They built an altar after another 500-mile journey to a new land. It was a land where they were strangers, a land promised to their offspring, but they had no offspring.

Surely they were in awe when God showed them the stars in the middle of the day and said, "You will have that many descendants." We know they laughed when God showed up at their tent and said, "In one year you will have a son." We know they laughed when Isaac was born. Then, this elderly, worn-out couple raised their long-promised son as best they could. They kept promises. They broke promises. It was messy.

Now, with Sarah's death, we feel the need to pause out of reverence for her life. She was named My Princess by her father and Mother of Many Nations by her God. Abraham went to her body, the wife with whom he had celebrated two golden anniversaries, and he wept. His body heaved with the sobs of such a great loss.

If you've been wondering how you could possibly fit into God's family with the losses you've experienced through death, divorce, or disappointment, I would say to you: This is us. Every family feels loss. Every family experiences broken promises. Abraham was not a perfect husband. He and Sarah did not have a perfect marriage. I say that just from what the Scriptures tell us. I don't know how stressful their moves were. I don't know how infertility affected their intimacy. I don't know if they agreed or disagreed about how to handle Lot, their nephew. I do know they experienced stress, disappointment, and loss. Just like us.

Brokenness

You might think that surely Genesis 23 could have been left out. God's promise had been fulfilled in Genesis 22. Abraham's story would be passed to the next generation in Genesis 24. Essentially all that happened in Genesis 23 was that Sarah died. So, why was an entire chapter devoted to it?

Genesis 23 enables us to see and to stop and to understand. The first family, God's family, is just like ours. When we lose people, the losses become as much a part of the story as all the gains. This chapter reminds us of an important truth:

Vows do not exempt us from brokenness.

It seems like a strange thing to say. Vows mean that things are held together. Vows give strength. Vows form foundations. Vows are something you can count on. But there's a reason vows need to be renewed: People we love do things we can't explain. *We* do things we can't explain and things we regret.

Earlier in their story, Sarai said to Abram, "The LORD has kept me from having children. Go, sleep with my slave; perhaps I can build a family through her" (Genesis 16:2).

Huh? She said what? She wouldn't do that.

She did it.

Let's not excuse Abram here either. The next line in the Scripture says "Abram agreed to what Sarai said."

Way to think it over for a minute, big boy. Can you imagine how much that messed up their marriage? Can you imagine how much that messed up their lives? Yes! Some of us can!

Don't mistake "Vows do not exempt us from brokenness" to mean "We all mess up; no big deal." Wrong! It means we all mess up, and it is a big deal! Breaking promises has repercussions for generations. Vows don't exempt us from brokenness, because people in covenant relationships do things we can't explain, things we regret. You can almost count on it.

Brokenness can lead to all kinds of things: despair, depression, and on and on. It can lead us to run away from our problems. But here is another important truth:

Brokenness can lead us to deeper intimacy.

Pretty crazy, huh? In God's family we let brokenness drive us closer to God. Some extreme situations, such as abuse, don't allow for this, but in many cases it's true. Why? Because a vow was made. Abraham and Sarah made a vow, and despite the brokenness they kept going forward. They teach us yet another important truth:

Intimacy does not exempt us from honor.

I have found that the closer people get, the less they tend to honor each other. The most obvious example is in a romantic relationship. On the first date we open the door and pull out the chair. We listen and engage and ask questions. But the closer we get to each other, the more we let our guard down, the more we show sides of ourselves that we don't show anyone else. There is something so good about that: authenticity. But surely it's possible to be authentic while still honoring the other. Those of us in God's family are called to honor each other—not just in our close relationships but with everyone. We are to listen and speak with honor.

Abraham told the Hittites—those in the land where Sarah had died—that he would like to buy a tomb. They replied, "Sir, listen to us. You are a mighty prince among us. Bury your dead in the choicest of our tombs. None of us will refuse you his tomb for burying your dead" (Genesis 23:6).

Abraham said, "I will pay for the tomb."

The Hittites said, "We will give it to you."

Still Abraham demanded to pay. He gave them four hundred shekels. He did not want a free tomb.

Why? Because of honor. Because of Sarah.

In God's Family

In God's family, honor leads to a deeper experience of love.

Closeness and intimacy do not mean we neglect honor. The closer we become, the more we should honor each other, so that we find a deeper experience of love. It's the same with God. We aren't supposed to be afraid of God, but we should fear God. We honor God. And as we honor God, we come closer to God. And here's where it gets weird:

In God's family, deeper love does not exempt us from loss.

In fact, the opposite is true. The more deeply we love, the more we lose. Abraham and Sarah took it all the way to the end, and when she died, Abraham wept and mourned. You may be hurting today, and if you are, it may be because you took the risk of love. In God's family, that's the way it works.

The promises of God include great loss. If you are weeping and mourning right now, you are in the line of Father Abraham and Mother Sarah. God's promise to them was a bigger family. Guess what? Bigger family, bigger loss.

The temptation is to isolate ourselves. After we've been burned a few times, after we've experienced loss, we are tempted to move away from other people. Many, many biblical characters chose isolation when the pain came. (Moses, Jonah, and Jacob are just a few.) But in the family of God, in times of loss we are called to come closer.

In John 11, Jesus lived this out. We are told that someone named Lazarus was sick. He wasn't just any man. He was Jesus' friend. He was Martha's brother. You remember Martha—when Jesus came to her house, she made preparations while her sister Mary sat at Jesus' feet. And Lazarus was their brother.

It makes sense, then, that people got word to Jesus by saying, "Lord, the one you love is sick" (John 11:3). They didn't even give his name. Not "Hey! Lazarus isn't feeling well. Next time you're through, give us a shout." No, they said, "Lord, the one you love is sick." We know what they were saying: Come, Jesus! Lazarus is dying! We need you!

It is in this story that we find the famous line, "Jesus wept." It turned out that Jesus didn't make it in time to see Lazarus still alive. Lazarus died. Jesus cried. He was deeply moved. He saw Mary crying. He saw everyone crying. He was too late. And Jesus wept. Perhaps Jesus' tears over Lazarus were not unlike Abraham's tears over Sarah.

In God's family, life is messy and we experience loss. In God's family, we can say "I believe" and "I don't understand" in the same breath. Maybe you've been taught that to be a Christian, you need to have it all figured out—perfect faith, not a twinge of doubt. Whoever taught you that was not reading our family story. Our story says that no matter what loss we experience or how bad it hurts, Jesus cares.

Renewing Vows

In God's family, loss leads to a renewal of vows.

When Lazarus died, Jesus did not isolate himself; he renewed relationships and promises by bringing life where we saw only death. When we read that Abraham buried Sarah, the very next story is about a marriage—of Isaac and Rebekah. Abraham longed for Isaac to experience the intimacy and vows and promises he had known with Sarah. And so:

*Isaac brought her into the tent of his mother
Sarah, and he married Rebekah. So she became
his wife, and he loved her; and Isaac was
comforted after his mother's death.*

(Genesis 24:67)

In the family of God we don't give up on love. God won't give up on us. We go through tough stuff, and we renew our vows.

When I was seventeen, I ran away from God for the first time, one of my first forays into the now-familiar territory of isolation. I stopped going to church. Some people at church sent me a note saying they missed me. I remember flinging it across my bedroom. Who were they to say that? I felt like they were getting into my business. What I forgot, of course, was that I had made a vow in front of all of them. I had promised not just to serve Jesus, but to serve him in union with the church that Jesus had opened to all people. All people included those people.

They didn't give up on me. One day my youth pastor, a guy we called Craig-O, came to my house while I was away and walked right into my bedroom. (My room had an outside entrance. Tip for parents: Not necessarily a good idea.) Technically Craig-O was breaking and entering, but there was a good result. On a notepad by my bed where I journaled, he wrote these words:

"He not busy being born is busy dying." —Craig-O

The quotation was actually not original to Craig-O. He knew that I knew it was a quotation from a Bob Dylan song. What was Craig saying to me? Something like this: "You made a promise, buddy. Not just to God, but to me. And whatever brokenness or loss you are experiencing as a seventeen-year-old, whatever is going on, I honor you."

He honored me enough to pursue me. I prayed that day and renewed my vows. I'm convinced that having Craig-O keep his side of the promise changed my life and possibly saved it.

So, I ask you today as a part of the family of God: Do you want to renew your vows?

5

Promise Maker and Promise Keeper

5

PROMISE MAKER AND PROMISE KEEPER

Jake made a promise. He was only six years old, but after I met with him over the course of a few months, I felt that he really did understand the promise.

It's difficult sometimes as a pastor to know what age is too young to be baptized. People have different thoughts on how old you need to be to understand the promises being made. I admit that six years old is pretty young to get it, but I also don't think any of us truly understands baptism. It is a step of faith, whether you're six years old or sixty. So as Jake's pastor, along with his parents, I felt that Jake was ready.

Little Jake stood before the church and made the promise, which was really a bunch of promises. He rejected evil. He repented of his sin. He promised to serve Jesus as Lord. His first-grade voice audibly articulated what his heart believed to be true. He was baptized, and the promises were sealed in his heart.

My hope and prayer is that Jake will keep those promises and will live a great life of faith in the family of God. Yet I know, because our story tells us so, that even the most faithful promise-makers will at times break the promises. Jake will inevitably fall short, forget, and fail, because we are part of a family of promise makers, promise keepers, and, yes, promise breakers.

Abraham's Growing Legacy

Our God is a promise maker and a promise keeper. God will be faithful to the promises even when we are not.

As someone who grew up in the 1990s, I can still quote most episodes of *Seinfeld*. That TV show depicts a different type of family from the classic sitcoms of earlier decades. Four single people in New York City live out life together in an environment that's quite different from that of the Cleavers or even the Bunkers. But, like any family, they learn about promises made, promises kept, and promises broken.

In one of my favorite episodes, Jerry and Elaine go to pick up a rental car at the airport. Jerry has made a reservation for a midsize car, but when he arrives he is told there are no midsize cars available. Jerry, confused, asks the woman at the desk if she understands what a reservation is. The lady says yes, of course she does. Jerry explains that she may know how to take a reservation, but she doesn't know how to *hold* the reservation. In Jerry's opinion, the holding is the most important part.

The scene reminds me of our propensity to make promises and then break them. But God is different. God is a promise maker and a promise keeper. God knows how to take the reservation and how to hold the reservation.

After Sarah died, Abraham remarried. Yes, you read that right. In spite of his incredibly long, happy first marriage, Abraham married again. He kept going. He kept promising. And then, after some time, Abraham died. His two sons, half-brothers Isaac and Ishmael, buried him next to Sarah.

Isaac married Rebekah, and in what seems to have been the first reported ultrasound reading, they learned from ultrasound tech God that Rebekah was pregnant with twins. They had two sons, Esau who came first, and Jacob who came right on his heels—literally. Jacob was holding Esau's heel, which is how he got the name Jacob. It means heel grabber or deceiver.

The theme was repeated as the twins grew up. Jacob tricked Esau out of his birthright. Complications arose, because Isaac liked Esau best and Rebekah liked Jacob best. Esau married two women, and Isaac and Rebekah didn't like them.

That's just a snapshot of Abraham's growing legacy, but you see what a mess it was: remarriage, a gaggle of siblings, conflict among family members, in-laws who didn't like in-laws. This is us? Yes, this is us.

Jacob's Ladder

It's clear that the mess of Abraham and Sarah got passed down, because we can see it in their offspring. In fact, if we're not careful, all we see in that family will be the bad stuff. We can feel the weight of that bad stuff in our own lives. Our family's mess is all around us. We say what they say and act like they act. It turns out that God's family is just like ours.

Well, hold on.

Jacob left his family and set out by himself for Harran (Genesis 28:10). Remember Harran? It was the place where Abraham had stalled out on his journey to Canaan. Jacob, because of all his tricking and deceiving, was now taking the same trail Abraham had traveled, but in the opposite direction. Along the way, Jacob stopped for the night and fell asleep, using a stone for a pillow. Do you recall what Abraham used stones for? Not pillows, but altars.

It was there, sleeping on the ground with the prospect of a sore neck in the morning, that Jacob dreamed of a heavenly stairway from heaven to earth, with angels going up and down upon it. Jacob, though he may have felt far from God, dreamed of a connection with God, a passageway between heaven and earth. This dream is often called Jacob's ladder. In it, God said,

> "I am the LORD, the God of your father
> Abraham and the God of Isaac. I will give you
> and your descendants the land on which you
> are lying. Your descendants will be like the dust
> of the earth, and you will spread out to the west
> and to the east, to the north and to the south.
> All peoples on earth will be blessed through
> you and your offspring. I am with you and will

watch over you wherever you go, and I will
bring you back to this land. I will not leave you
until I have done what I have promised you."

(Genesis 28:13-15)

Whoa. God made a promise to Jacob that was virtually the same as the one he gave to Abraham. As Jacob traveled to Harran, God reminded him of the promise he gave to Abraham when he was to leave Harran: I will give you this land. Your descendants will be like dust. All people on earth will be blessed through you. God has not given up on the promise. God will not give up on the promise.

When Jacob woke up, he knew that he had been in the presence of the Lord. As the sun rose, he took the stone he had used for a pillow, poured oil on it, and made an altar, just as Grandpa had done. Surely Jacob had been told his whole life about God's promise to Father Abraham in Harran. The story was in Jacob's brain, in his heart, in his bones. It had been passed down to him. And now here he was, running away from that promise, and God met him right there.

Then Jacob made a vow, saying, "If God will
be with me and will watch over me on this
journey I am taking and will give me food to
eat and clothes to wear so that I return safely
to my father's household, then the Lord *will be*
my God."

(Genesis 28:20-21)

In taking that vow, Jacob the promise breaker became Jacob the promise maker and promise keeper. Up to that point Jacob had basically been bratty and spoiled, and that is putting it nicely. We could also say he had been deceptive and destructive. That same Jacob, inspired by a dream, was pursued by God into the desert and down through the years.

God Passes Down Dreams

You want to know your heritage? Look at dreams. God's people are dreamers. I don't always know what do with dreams—either my own or the dreams of others. As a pastor, people often share their dreams with me. If I'm honest, I often don't know what to do with the dreams. But even though the dreams aren't always clear and I don't often know the next step, the dreams give me joy. When I hear that we are still dreaming, I remember the family I belong to, the family of people who have no business dreaming and yet keep dreaming the promises of God.

I'll fast-forward in our story just a bit so we can see how this promise-making God kept dreams in the forefront of God's family. Jacob had a bunch of sons—twelve, in fact—but, like his parents before him, Jacob seemed to have a favorite child. The child's name was Joseph. And, you guessed it, Joseph had a dream. His dream was a doozy, especially for someone with eleven brothers.

Jacob, the doting father, gave Joseph an ornate robe, a coat of many colors that was like a neon sign flashing "Dad's favorite."

Joseph, in turn, would bring back reports to his father about his older brothers. You get the picture. Joseph was a tattletale with a fancy jacket from Dad, and as a result he was not highly thought of by his jealous brothers. The Scriptures say that Joseph's brothers could not speak a kind word to him.

That's when Joseph started dreaming. He dreamed that he and his brothers were out binding sheaves of grain in the field, and his sheaf stood upright while his brothers' sheaves bowed down to him. And he shared the dream with his brothers. Seriously!

He had another dream, and he shared that one, too. In his dream the sun and moon (representing his mother and father) and eleven stars (his eleven brothers) bowed down to Joseph. This was too much even for Jacob. Jacob asked, "What is this dream you had? Will your mother and I and your brothers actually come and bow down to the ground before you?" (Genesis 37:10).

Dreaming of Greatness

Pause for a moment and try to remember a time in your life when you dreamed of greatness. Try to remember what it felt like to hold the bursting hope and belief that you could do and be something great. Maybe you held on to that dream for a long time, or maybe it was snuffed out quickly.

I remember when I put on my first Little League uniform. I thought I could be like my major league heroes, who could see a curveball coming from a mile away. It turned out I couldn't hit a ball thrown underhanded slowly. But I dreamed, and maybe you did too.

Sure, Joseph seemed bratty and spoiled, but he also had a purity of his heart in imagining that God could use him for something great. Surely some of us could use a dose of that.

However, Joseph's brothers were so hurt and offended by Joseph and his dreams that one day, when Joseph came to check on them in the distant fields, they devised a plan to kill him.

> *"Here comes that dreamer!" they said to each other. "Come now, let's kill him and throw him into one of these cisterns and say that a ferocious animal devoured him. Then we'll see what comes of his dreams."*
>
> *(Genesis 37:19-20)*

Instead of killing him, though, the brothers ended up showing Joseph a measure of compassion. They stripped off his coat and threw him into a cistern. A cistern is a pit. There are still many in that part of that world. They hold water. They are fifteen to twenty feet deep and made of solid rock, almost like a small cave.

The brothers then sold Joseph into slavery and cooked up a cover up story for their father saying that Joseph had been killed. Jacob was beside himself with grief. The brothers lived with guilt. And, oh yeah, Joseph was riding away on a cart to become a slave in Egypt.

What does this have to do with you?

Your life is very different from Joseph's, but most of us have faced a mess caused by jealousy or conflict or immaturity or guilt or deceit or some combination of those. For example, my brother never threw me into a pit, but he did make me the official electric fence tester on the farm near where we grew up. I've never forgiven him for that. Okay, I'm kidding, but you get the idea. You've probably experienced something like that in your own relationships. They exist in most families, and they snuff out dreams.

Dreams vs. Reality

Joseph, son of a dreamer, great-grandson of a dreamer, teaches us that life usually turns out differently from how we dreamed it. There really is no blueprint for life. There is no glimpse of the end when you are at the beginning. That's not how life works; it's not how following Jesus works.

I think that instead of this being a negative, however, it can be one of the great positives of being on the adventure with God. We see the next step and take it but rarely see much further than that. Over and over again we dream, but we don't get to see what the dream will look like when it is fulfilled. When we finally do see, the dream often appears to be very different from our first conception of it. Spoiler alert: Joseph's dreams come true, but, as with our dreams, they look quite different from the way Joseph originally dreamed them.

Because of this truth about our dreams, we must learn to adjust our expectations. I'm being practical here, but also biblical. The main characters in God's messy family show us that we constantly must adjust our expectations regarding timing and promises. Life is about adjusting.

Our church recently lost a saint. His name was Bob. Bob was one of the gentlest, wisest, more faithful people I have ever known. Some months ago he received a difficult medical diagnosis. Afterward, as he and his wife Rita sat in the car in the doctor's office parking lot, Bob grabbed his wife's hand. Their expectations had changed drastically. He said, "This is life, and Jesus is in control." Bob had learned that life is about adjusting expectations while still trusting in Jesus, about believing the promise when we don't know how things will go. And it's really hard.

Yet, we are to live with integrity whether expectations are unmet, met, or exceeded. Joseph's life held all three. Yours will have all three. What we learn from Joseph is that our behavior, our faithfulness, our morality, and our interactions with others are not based on circumstance or expectations. We don't do what's right when things go the way we had hoped and then take out our frustrations on others when things go differently. What we learn from Joseph's story is to live with integrity and faithfulness in all seasons.

Joseph was thrown a big curveball in life, but once you've seen a curveball or two you're more likely to hit the next one. Joseph's life was filled with curveballs. He was thrown in a pit, sold as a slave, falsely accused of sexual harassment, wrongfully thrown in prison, and forgotten by those who said they would remember him. In spite of the curveballs, at the end of the story he offered a beautiful act of grace and reconciliation that led his brothers to fall down at his feet, just like in the dream. He could have acted with vengeance, but instead he used the changing expectations as opportunities to honor God. He trained himself with integrity in small moments, and that allowed him to act with integrity in his greatest moment.

And the craziest thing was that he didn't stop dreaming.

Don't stop dreaming. Why? Because when it comes to expectations, God's plan prevails. We can dream big and foolishly and wonderfully and leave it all in God's hands. That's what Joseph did. His father's name, Jacob, means to struggle, but Joseph's name means to add or increase. Joseph, struggling, continued to dream big and see God do big things.

God's Promise

One of my favorite verses is Proverbs 19:21, which says, "Many are the plans in a person's heart, / but it is the LORD's purpose that prevails." We dream all these dreams, and that's good, but we can be assured that in the end the Lord's purpose will prevail. This knowledge allows us to breathe deep and look for the view, even though the view isn't what we expected.

In God's family, everyone is invited to dream. When the church was formed with God's dynamic Holy Spirit through the power of Christ, it was said that young and old, men and women, dreamed. It's one way you know the church, because God's family dreams.

Abraham dreamed, Jacob dreamed, Joseph dreamed, and you will dream. God passes down dreams, and the dreams hold the promise. Remember the promise made to Abraham at Harran.

> The LORD had said to Abram, "Go from your
> country, your people and your father's household
> to the land I will show you.
>
> "I will make you into a great nation,
>   and I will bless you;
> I will make your name great,
>   and you will be a blessing.
> I will bless those who bless you,
>   and whoever curses you I will curse;
> and all peoples on earth
>   will be blessed through you."
>   (Genesis 12:1-3)

What was the promise to Jacob? Same promise. What was the promise to Joseph? Same promise. What is the promise to you? You see where I'm headed. God is making that same promise to you: greatness, blessing, and the ability pass it down.

Sure, we pass down bad stuff. It grieves us. We see our children's anxiety, and we recognize it as our own. We hear the sharp tongue of our teenagers, and we know where they learned it. My kids think bathroom humor is funny, and I know they learned it from their grandpa. Of course we pass down bad stuff, but what I want to tell you today is that those things are more like seeds sown than curses given. Yes, what comes before affects what comes after, but we are not bound by the stuff in our family's past. We see this in Jacob and Joseph. Sure, they carried the seeds of their forefathers' mess, but those seeds weren't a curse. Jacob, Joseph, and their families were able to live beautiful, God-given dreams.

No matter what has come before in our family heritage, we are not cursed. I'll tell you why: Jesus.

Jesus. Jesus. Jesus. Jesus. Curses are broken in Jesus. Hosea 8:7 says, "They sow the wind / and reap the whirlwind." Some of us are reaping the whirlwind, but we aren't bound by it. Our inheritance in Jesus is promise. So, don't become overly anxious about passing down your flaws. God is the only perfect parent, and you aren't God. What you truly get to pass down is God's promise.

Passing Down the Promise

I believe God wants to make and keep promises to you. I believe God wants you to dream.

You may think this is dumb, but my wife Rachel and I have a number through which we think God speaks to us, or maybe kind of winks at us. I have no biblical backing for this; it's just a way that Rachel and I are reminded of God's presence in our lives. The number is 129.

Genesis 29 is the chapter in which Jacob meets and marries Rachel. My name is Jacob and I married a Rachel, so that chapter is special for us. First book in the Bible: 1. Twenty-ninth chapter: 29. So 129.

When Rachel and I were seventeen, we used that number as our code when we paged each other. (Pagers? We are getting old.) One day a few years later, we walked past the kindergarten classroom where we met at First Baptist Church and saw that it was Room 129. We got married off that one! We've had several other instances of this over the years, including a baby born on January 29th. This may be silly, but it means something to us, and in it we feel God's promise making and promise keeping.

On the day the full solar eclipse passed through our town, we took our girls out of school and watched God put the moon in front of the sun in our front yard. The moon is four hundred times smaller than the sun, but it's four hundred times closer to the earth, so on rare occasions the disk of the moon perfectly covers the sun. This was one of those occasions, and we were there to see it. There's a moment in a solar eclipse when you can take your protective glasses off. We did and saw the craziest light show we had ever seen. My girls were going nuts. It was surreal. I looked at my watch to see how much time we had left to watch this crazy scene, and the time was 1:29 p.m. I showed Rachel, and we kissed and danced with our kids under stars in the middle of the day, just like Father Abraham and Mother Sarah. To be honest, we'd been working too hard and the kids had been really busy. We were going through a tough season in our lives and were trying to find a rhythm again. And as I stood under the stars at 1:29, I remembered God's promise: "I am with you and will watch over you wherever you go" (Genesis 28:15).

I believe we are a part of God's family, and God passes down to us good promises. I believe our heritage is a blessing and not a curse.

On the day of the solar eclipse, I got a call from Jake's dad. Remember Jake, the six-year-old who had been baptized? His dad called me and asked, "Can I get baptized with Jake?" And I said, "Yes, yes you can." Because that is our heritage. We make promises that we might not even fully understand. We certainly don't know how they will end up. But we promise anyway, just like our Father does.

Our God is a promise maker and a promise keeper. That God is with you and will watch over you wherever you go.

6

The Beauty
of Imperfection

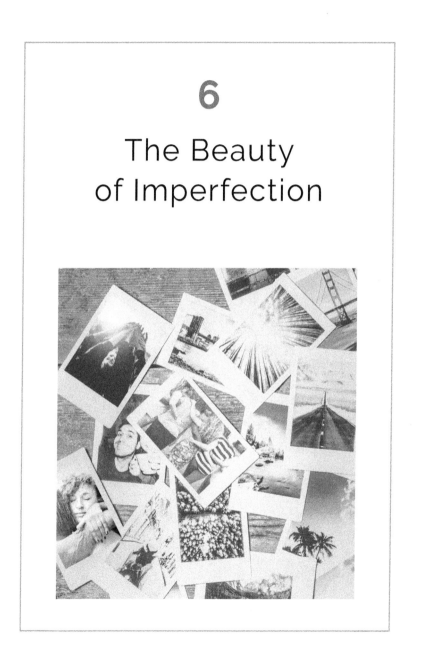

6

THE BEAUTY
OF IMPERFECTION

You think you have family issues? Joseph's family had thrown him into a pit!

But then a rope appeared. Joseph squinted and saw Simeon. He could hear Judah's voice. His brothers were pulling him out! Perhaps the nightmare was over. He reached the surface, and his eyes adjusted from darkness to the afternoon sun. There was Levi. There was Dan. His brothers hadn't left.

Quickly, though, Joseph realized they weren't alone. Strangely dressed foreigners were exchanging money with his brothers. Joseph recognized them as Midianite traders, merchants who traveled through his homeland from time to time. And then it hit him. The money being exchanged was for him. Joseph's brothers had sold him into slavery.

Expectations can change quickly. I thought life would look this way, but it went that way, and fast! I thought parenting would be like this, but oh, it is like that! I thought I would love this job, but I hate it. I thought my marriage would be great, but it has been disappointing. I thought I would be fulfilled, but I'm unfulfilled. I thought Mom would be with us forever, but we are losing her.

Joseph had dreamed of how his life would look. His brothers were supposed to bow down to him, but they had chained him up and sold him into slavery.

> *So when the Midianite merchants came by,*
> *his brothers pulled Joseph up out of the cistern*
> *and sold him for twenty shekels of silver to the*
> *Ishmaelites, who took him to Egypt.*
>
> *(Genesis 37:28)*

Joseph was an important part of God's messy family, and so we will pay close attention to his story, which covers fourteen chapters at the end of Genesis. Joseph was the son of Jacob and the great-grandson of Father Abraham. He was one of the central figures in our family of faith. And things would get worse for him before they got better.

"There's Something About This Guy"

The Midianite merchants, after arriving in Egypt, sold Joseph to Potiphar, a high-ranking Egyptian officer and captain of Pharaoh's royal guard. Potiphar saw something in Joseph. Like Jacob, Joseph's doting father, Potiphar thought, "There's something about this guy."

> *When his master saw that the LORD was with him and that the LORD gave him success in everything he did, Joseph found favor in his eyes and became his attendant. Potiphar put him in charge of his household, and he entrusted to his care everything he owned.*
> *(Genesis 39:3-4)*

Potiphar's wife also thought, "There's something about this guy." She took a liking to Joseph and invited him to come to bed with her. Joseph refused, knowing the depth of betrayal he would inflict if he slept with Potiphar's wife. Potiphar's wife, though, didn't give up. One day she caught Joseph by his coat and made her invitation again. Joseph again refused and tried to get away from her, but she grabbed his coat. (Joseph's coat continued to get him in trouble.) Coat in hand, Potiphar's wife walked straight to her husband and lied, saying Joseph tried to take advantage of her. And so Joseph went to prison.

Guess what happened in prison? The prison warden saw Joseph and thought, "There's something about this guy." The warden put Joseph in charge of all the prisoners. Amazing. Everywhere Joseph went, he seemed to rise to the top.

In prison, Joseph interpreted the dreams of two prisoners to help win their freedom. He asked the prisoners to remember him when they got out. But they forgot, and Joseph was left in prison.

Everywhere Joseph went, he was thrown into pits. Pits created by jealousy, by lust, by the selfishness of others. Joseph's relationships hurt him over and over again. But there was something about that guy . . .

Joseph's Story

We can hear Joseph's story and think, "What a crazy life!" But is it crazier than yours? It's got drama, for sure. But is it more dramatic than yours? The things that Joseph experienced were the very things we all experience in our messy relationships with others.

Joseph experienced betrayal.

Betrayal was big in Joseph's story. Potiphar's wife made a false accusation, and Potiphar put Joseph in prison without a trial. The guy whom Joseph helped get out of prison never spoke up on his behalf. The big betrayal, of course, was when Joseph's brothers sold him for a bag of silver. Now, I never met Joseph, but I guarantee that that one stuck with him. He thought of that one while he wore Egyptian clothes in a land that was not his own. He thought of that one as he tried to sleep on the hard prison floor.

Betrayal is an expectation-buster. We all experience betrayals, both big and small. Some of us experience them in our own family, with the people we thought loved us most. Wherever we meet betrayal, it's hard to shake.

Joseph experienced bondage.

Joseph was a favored son. He had the special coat. He walked around telling people about his dreams of greatness. Contrast that with being tied and bound and transported to a foreign country. Joseph went from being the golden boy to being a slave and then a convict.

Most of us don't know that kind of bondage, but we know what it feels like to be weighted down and chained up. Maybe it's caused by an addiction or a depression or a wound that won't heal. As with Joseph, some of the things holding us in bondage were imposed by our family, and some are completely beyond our control. Do you know bondage? What has tied you up?

Joseph was blindsided.

To be blindsided is to get hit hard when you don't see it coming. It can happen while you're playing quarterback, while you're driving, or while you're leading a normal, everyday life.

Joseph was blindsided. He walked out to the fields to check on his brothers, and he was thrown into a pit. Working in the home of Potiphar, his coat was pulled off and he was thrown in prison.

Being blindsided has an effect on our heart. The unexpected phone call, the bad news, the surprise death—these things leave a mark. They make us defensive, insecure, and anxious. Have you been blindsided?

Joseph was abandoned.

I know, you thought they would all start with *B*! Believe me, I tried! In the South, where I'm from, abandoned sort of sounds like it starts with a *B*. You know—'bandoned. I'm never gonna make it in this business.

Joseph was abandoned in the bottom of a pit and then later in life waited in prison for someone to remember him. One way or another, we've all experienced that. The betrayals, the bondage, the blindside hits—all these things leave us feeling that we've been forgotten and abandoned. We are left to figure things out on our own. If you've been in relationships with people for any length of time, you've experienced the feeling of being alone.

In God's messy family we experience betrayal, bondage, blindside hits, and abandonment. But there's more to it than that. We can easily confuse the way people have treated us with the way God is treating us.

God Is with Us

God has not abandoned you, not then, not now, not ever. You have not been left alone, have not been left to figure things out on your own, and have not been forgotten. Joseph's beautiful story teaches us there is no place we can go and nothing we can experience that will separate us from God.

Everywhere Joseph went, God went with him.

Joseph was thrown into a pit, and the Lord was with him. In a pit!

Joseph was sold into slavery, and the Lord was with him. In Egypt!

Joseph was thrown into prison, and the Lord was with him. In prison!

In fact, it's an ongoing theme in Joseph's story: people forget Joseph, but God never forgets. This is true for all of us in God's messy family. It's why I can promise you right now, no matter what it feels like, that God is with you. Hang on. Hang in. God will not abandon you.

Joseph experienced all the things we experience, and he remained faithful regardless of circumstances. When bad circumstances arise, we can shake our fist at the sky. We can be frustrated, hurt, or angry. But it's no time to abandon God, because God won't abandon us. When Joseph was a servant, he served to the glory of God. When Joseph was a prisoner, he used his captivity to point others to God. Joseph did what was right even when things weren't going right for him.

Remember my job at the feed store, when I swept in the meantime? It turns out that the meantime is most of the time; so if we're waiting for some grand moment when everything will be clean and neat, we'll be waiting a long time.

Joseph had dreamed of greatness. He kept thinking it was right around the corner, just on the horizon. Though Joseph didn't know it, his waiting was almost over.

Joseph Revealed

Two years later, Pharaoh had a dream, and one of the prisoners whom Joseph had helped was part of Pharaoh's court.

The man told Pharaoh about Joseph, and Pharaoh sent for him. Joseph, with God's help, correctly interpreted the dream.

Pharaoh needed someone to manage food production, storage, and disbursement during the following seven years of abundance and seven years of famine. And Pharaoh, like Joseph's father, slave master, and prison warden, thought, "There's something about this guy."

> *So Pharaoh said to Joseph, "I hereby put you in charge of the whole land of Egypt." Then Pharaoh took his signet ring from his finger and put it on Joseph's finger. He dressed him in robes of fine linen and put a gold chain around his neck. He had him ride in a chariot as his second-in-command, and people shouted before him, "Make way!" Thus he put him in charge of the whole land of Egypt.*
>
> (Genesis 41:41-43)

In this new position of honor and power, Joseph saved the known world around Egypt. He saved the king. He saved the prison warden and his prison buddies. He saved Potiphar and Potiphar's wife. And, you guessed it, he saved his rascally brothers.

During the famine, Joseph's father learned there was grain in Egypt and sent his sons to get some food so the family wouldn't die. When Joseph's brothers arrived, they stood before Joseph, the governor of the land.

And they bowed down to him.

Joseph, of course, knew they were his brothers, but they didn't know he was Joseph. In fact, they even told Joseph that one of their brothers had died! Then they spoke among each other in their native language, not knowing he could understand them. Joseph was so affected by it all that he retreated into a private room and cried his eyes out.

Joseph didn't reveal himself at that first meeting, but through a series of events his brothers came back, including the youngest, Benjamin.

> *Then Joseph could no longer control himself*
> *before all his attendants, and he cried out,*
> *"Have everyone leave my presence!" So there*
> *was no one with Joseph when he made himself*
> *known to his brothers. And he wept so loudly*
> *that the Egyptians heard him, and Pharaoh's*
> *household heard about it. . . .*
>
> *Then he threw his arms around his brother*
> *Benjamin and wept, and Benjamin embraced*
> *him, weeping. And he kissed all his brothers and*
> *wept over them.*
>
> (Genesis 45:1-2, 14-15)

Joseph's father even came to see him. Jacob, now called Israel, traveled to see the son he thought was dead. Anybody want to guess what happened?

> *As soon as Joseph appeared before him, he threw*
> *his arms around his father and wept for a long*
> *time.*
>
> *(Genesis 46:29)*

They all lived together for seventeen years before Jacob died. When he did, the brothers became afraid, concerned that now Joseph would take out his revenge. They came before him and threw themselves on the ground. In response, Joseph gave them a line that we could spend many days pondering. He said,

> *"You intended to harm me, but God intended it*
> *for good to accomplish what is now being done,*
> *the saving of many lives."*
>
> *(Genesis 50:20)*

What We Can Expect

When Joseph saw all the mess, all the hurt, all the tears of his family, he viewed it in the context of how God could and would work among them. Joseph saw his inclusion in God's messy family as an opportunity for God to use him to do good.

What do we learn from Joseph that we can expect in God's messy family?

Expect many tears.

Expect tears and tears and tears and tears. I can't go with the TV preachers who promise only prosperity and happiness.

I don't know anyone who followed God more faithfully than Joseph, and his life was a river of tears. Even as beautiful things were happening, he carried the grief of the prison floor and the betrayal of the pit.

I have to tell you, the longer I follow Jesus, the more I cry. Last year I lost a dear friend to cancer. In the year since his loss, I have cried a river of tears. I saw his wife a few weeks ago after church, and I had something I wanted to tell her. Instead I just cried. She just cried. This crazy life with God has tears. It has the good ones and the hard ones. Regularly people at church come up to me crying. Often they apologize for their tears. I tell them I'm thankful that church is the place where those tears will enter the world. Tears, after all, are part of being in the family.

Expect so much forgiveness.

We need a well of forgiveness. You can almost see the moments when Joseph wanted to exact revenge on his rascally brothers. They sold him into slavery. They tricked their dad into thinking he was dead. And so Joseph would cry and forgive and cry and forgive, until the forgiveness flowed like the tears. Joseph knew that the forgiveness was for them and their freedom, but also for him and his freedom. If he didn't forgive, he was still in bondage. If he didn't forgive, he was still a prisoner.

It's true for us, too. If we don't forgive, we stay chained up. Our lives are messy and crazy and we have to forgive. We find the forgiveness in Jesus.

God can take what others meant for harm and
use it to save lives.

Joseph's story doesn't teach us that God makes bad things so
good can come out of it. No, that would be a scary kind of God.
But God can take what others mean for harm and use it to save
lives. If God can't do that, we need to convert our churches into
coffee shops or community centers. Both are good things. But
God's family isn't about coffee and good deeds. It's about a God
who has the power to save us. It's about a God who can take the
bad that others have done to us and use it to save our lives and
the lives of others.

You never know what God might be up to!

That's what Joseph teaches us. It's why I say over and over
again: Hang on. Hang in. It's what I put a message on repeat:
Don't give up. It's why we all have to keep on sweeping.

But God . . .

The statement that God's family must claim is simple and
short. It is this:

But God . . .

Joseph said to his brothers, "You intended to harm me, but
God intended it for good to accomplish what is now being done,
the saving of many lives." But God.

Joseph's brothers wanted to sell him into slavery, but God
had a different idea. Potiphar's wife wanted Joseph in prison, but

God was working the whole time. Joseph probably expected to live out his days an official in Egypt, but God had in mind to reconcile Joseph's family.

What is your story? What do you look at and think: Why did this happen in my life? What can God do?

Yes, our family is messy. Yes, it has its share of betrayal and abandonment. But we don't give up. Through us, God intends to save as many things and many people we thought were lost. So stay in it. Stay in the story. Stay in the promises spoken over Abraham. They are the same promises being spoken over us.

And now the family, our family, has been thrown wide open. In Jesus it's no longer limited to the descendants of Abraham. Now all of us can claim Father Abraham. We are the people of his promise. This is us.

CONCLUSION

Ty was over at our house the other night. You remember, Ty, Tamirat Yishak, our "miracle" from Ethiopia who laughs like his namesake Isaac. It was the same scene that is usually present when Ty and his family join us. Kids are running around, food is being consumed, the house is being destroyed. There is much laughter, much joy, but it's real and really chaotic. As the evening was winding down and shoes and socks were being found and all the kids were being found, I saw Ty speaking with my wife Rachel. She was bending over and listening carefully to what Ty had to say. Sometimes Ty talks really loud, other times very soft. and I could tell this was one of those moments when Rachel had to lean close to make out his soft-spoken words.

Ty was telling Rachel about some baby birds that had recently hatched in a nest in our front yard. To Ty this was very important business and I could tell Rachel was taking it seriously. I walked out with Ty to see what had him so concerned about these new hatchlings. The sun had already set, but there was enough light for me to see the issue at hand. A little baby bird had found its way out of the nest and was sitting on a window sill. He could fly a little, but not enough to make a true escape into his new world. The bird seemed to be quite afraid and unsure about what to do next.

Ty is eight years old now. I was able to see the moment in a "slow" way even with all that was going on. I was proud of him. He is strong now and intelligent and perceptive while in many ways he is still acclimating to a new world of his own some seven years later. I was thankful to be on the journey with him. I am only a small piece of his family, but I know an important one and for that I am grateful. It's hard for me to see it through my love for him, but like all of us Ty is imperfect and fragile himself. I am committed to walking through the journey with him while God gives me opportunity. Ty who had experienced rescue in his life was now seeing himself as the rescuer.

It seems God is always taking us into new lands, giving us new dreams, and reminding us of old promises. Like Ty, it takes time to get acclimated to the new territory to which God brings us. It usually takes longer than we thought it would. If we aren't careful we will see only our imperfections and have our vision clouded by fear. We feel vulnerable and fragile. We are in danger of missing the good things God is offering us. What are those good things? Well, the old promises to be sure, the family stories that must be shared, the gifting that we didn't even know we had, but mostly . . . each other. The blessing of each other. The blessing of entering the new territory together. The blessing of family.

Old Jacob is revived when he hears that his son Joseph is alive and has sent for him to come to Egypt. Jacob sets out for Egypt and God tells him that, "Guess what?," God will go with him to Egypt (the same old promise!). Jacob is still being sent into new lands even as he nears the end of his life.

Joseph couldn't wait. He had his chariot made ready and rode out to Jacob as he traveled to Egypt. "As soon as Joseph appeared before [Jacob], he threw his arms around his father and wept for a long time" (Genesis 46:29). I'll just let that verse speak for itself.

And then, before Jacob dies, he blesses all his sons. In Genesis 49, Jacob gives a specific and appropriate blessing to all twelve sons. He does not just have a blessing for the firstborn. He does not just have blessing for the sons who did not trick him. Jacob, the chief deceiver himself, gives them one and all a blessing. He saw them, he spoke to them, and he gave them a blessing. He knew they still had many more lands to walk into. He knew their imperfections and he loved them just the same.

In the same way, God sees us, knows us, speaks to us, and offers us blessings. In the lineage of Abraham, Isaac, and Jacob, and Sarah, Rebekah, and Rachel, God loves us one and all. God is ushering us into new lands that take a long time to get used to. In vulnerability and fragility, God makes promises. So, do not be afraid. God really wants to heal you, secure you, and use you in the story. It is a good story, with a good family, because it is a good God. Keep walking and remember you do not go alone.

I wish I could tell you the fate of the baby bird. I let Ty and my daughter Phoebe handle it. Another child needed my attention and I entrusted the escaped bird to my eight-year-old progeny. It sounds scary, I know, but I trust them. Hopefully we have passed down enough blessing to those two that they don't always see themselves as vulnerable and fragile, but they know that they are responsible to the vulnerable and fragile. I imagine there is a good story behind how they rescued the bird and put it in its rightful safe place for more growth and maturity. Or maybe one day I will hear another story that is more like brothers throwing their baby brother in a pit, I don't know. But, I look forward to the story, because it's my family story. My family story involves the imperfect and the broken. But, it also includes the restored children of promise. It's messy, but I wouldn't have it any other way. And, I know this: we, the people of God, are abundantly blessed as we walk into new lands together.

ACKNOWLEDGMENTS

To Ron Kidd who has walked with me through ten books or more. You were always patient, always kind, and never kept a record of deadlines missed. Sounds a lot like love. Thank you, Ron. Best wishes as you write for another generation.

To William, Mary Elizabeth, Wilbur, and Kay. Thank you for welcoming me into a messy, beautiful family. You made many sacrifices and I'm sure many mistakes. You covered them over with love, grace, and promise. You guys remind me of the great patriarchs and matriarchs of the Bible. I am proud to be your grandson and look forward to telling all the stories when we are together again.

To Rachel, it feels like every story I write, you write with me. The best part of my life is sharing it with you. Thanks for letting me write books, believe in big dreams, and mostly for loving me like Sarah loved Abraham, a love that builds altars to God.

Jesus, I acknowledge you. Thanks for holding the pen and I hope typing the keys while I write. Your story is the one that captivates me and grips my heart. Your love saves a seat for me at the family table. It is all for you.

The Connected Life
Small Groups That Create Community

This handy and helpful guide describes how churches can set up, maintain, and nurture small groups to create a congregation that is welcoming and outward-looking.

Written by founding pastor Jacob Armstrong with Rachel Armstrong, the guide is based on the pioneering small group ministry of Providence United Methodist Church in Mt. Juliet, Tennessee.

978-1-5018-4345-7

978-1-5018-4346-4 eBook

 **Abingdon Press**™

Available wherever fine books are sold.

CPSIA information can be obtained
at www.ICGtesting.com
Printed in the USA
LVHW081111241118
597827LV00005BA/7/P